PROLAPSE

OFF THE PARK PRESS NEW YORK, NEW YORK 2011

RONNA LEBO

PROLAPSE

Cover image: *Prolapse,* 2008
Oil on canvas by Ronna Lebo
Painting 32 x 24 inches

Book design by Shari DeGraw

ISBN 978-0-9791495-2-8

Printed on acid-free paper
in the United States of America

To contact the press, please write

OFF THE PARK PRESS
73 FIFTH AVENUE, 8B
NEW YORK, NEW YORK 10003

Off The Park Press books
are distributed by SPD

SMALL PRESS DISTRIBUTION
1341 SEVENTH STREET
BERKELEY, CALIFORNIA 94710

1-800-869-7553
orders@spdbooks.org
www.spdbooks.org

to Dan Dermond,
free forever from addiction,
torment and the loving
family that killed him.
(1964-2008)

CONTENTS

ALIDADE

FLORIDA

Florida turns in today's yard; a slow spin on white pebbles next to a tuft or two of brown seagrass; an exercise assigned in therapy to contact the earth through bare feet. She holds her stilettos by their backstraps, one hooked on each index finger. She spins then stops, knowing certainly that this movement is therapy wasted. She has no future plans or the means to change herself. Her eyes are red: not the rims; those are painted black, and not the whites; those are white with blue under-neath. She is the mother of two sons. Her favorite word is "you."

Florida makes her way to the hot pavement and straps herself back into her heels. There will be no more touching the earth with her bare soles ever again.

MARTIN

Martin doesn't like his brother, doesn't much like his dad, either. He prefers his mother's side of the bed where the flowers bend down. His dad sleeps on the couch, so his parent's room is a vacation where Martin dreams of his mother and her missing.

The original plan had been for him to leave with the baby and father, coming home to visit once a month: Things change rapidly when Florida and the weather are involved.

FLORIDA

The woman is Florida, slick and violent. She melts the wall as she passes.
In her estimation there are lines and edges where ceilings and floors meet.
She does not acknowledge that these edges disagree to meet when she erases
a wall by passing.

Sweat forms along the upper lip when contemplating a dialogue with her before
realizing there will be no dialogue. Her hair is bleach-white. Her underarms smell
of rage and perfume. Her steps mince along the hall due to the height of her
heels and the length of her skirt. She will humiliate one son at four o'clock, and
his father later at 8:00 pm. Neither one of them will look closely at her while she
speaks. She has learned interrogation skills from a specific training camp.

MARTIN AND FLORIDA

There is an imprint on the bed where her body used to lay. Brown and yellow flowers on the spread ripple and roll minutely downward, then up again where they meet the ridges of mattress indented by his mother. Martin knows she is not there, but carefully lays himself inside the contours of her imprint, imagines her cool warmth and feels held. She never held him, but this is better than the real her. It is his secret mother. She arrived the day after she left.

DEREK

Derek hits the brakes hard and the baby squeals in its seat, a little high-pitched choking. He wonders if he can make the kid do that again. He hits the brakes – Nope, no squeal. This boy looks too much like his wife. The kid has a balloon face and a dumb intention in his eyes. His eyes are almost red – even though they are green. Derek wishes to high hell that Florida had taken this one away with her.

She'd come back from some therapy session or another, packed and said she was taking everything the children needed for the rest of their lives. There was a quick succession of heated sentences ending with the abrupt change that left him with the house and kids. Derek wished now that he had negotiated the disappearance of at least this son, specifically.

DEREK AND FLORIDA

Derek and Florida met in Korea, at a club where she stripped. Florida knew not to expect much more from her current lifestyle. They were an unlikely pair, but she was ready to leave and Derek was infatuated enough to take her home with him. She wanted asylum as a housewife. They shipped out to Miami first, then to a small suburb in North Carolina, where first one son was born, and six years later, another.

Their street was named San Lucas, and the next parallel street was Borneo, where a strip mall enticed local teens and drug dealers to score. The view from the western-most window of Florida's bedroom was a constant reminder of supply-and-demand engagements. The easternmost window in the den at the opposite end of the house looked out onto another street, Canary Isle, at the end of which one could imagine the sound.

DEREK

Florida is corseted in her bag. She no longer looks real, but then she is not alive. State troopers located her body behind a Mexican take-out in Ohio, thrown recklessly on top of a dumpster. Her murderers evidently did not worry about appearances. The police have notified Derek that the investigation is ongoing, but there is little evidence to gather. No one at the restaurant remembers Florida, and no reports from adjacent states have been forthcoming after her picture was posted in the local news.

MARTIN

Martin dreams of flying over the rooftops carried in Florida's arms. He is tiny
and she is a giant on the sky. Her white hands hold his head and ankles tightly –
stretched out in front of her as she soars at a sickening speed forever forward
into the clouds. In this dream, Martin is terrified that she will drop him, but at the
same time he feels the secure grasp of her fingers tighten. The grip she is holding
his head within slowly shifts to a choking sensation in his throat. He wakes up
20   crying.

FLORIDA

Florida is dead and invisible. Even her sons have stopped knowing who she is. Her driver's license was found in the recycling bin next to the dumpster where her body was left. It had been easy to trace her back to North Carolina. All Derek remembers feeling during the initial police notification was annoyance that she'd never be able to take that kid off his hands.

MARTIN

He remembers spying on her when she was angry, sneaking around to watch where she was, stay out of her way. There was a day he watched her wreck a chair with a pair of scissors, which she later blamed on the dog. That dog had run away. She said she saw it dead on the highway on her way to the Super Shop. Nothing stopped the huge love he carried for her in his heart. To Martin, his mother was an horrible angel sent to bleach his world. He felt reassured knowing she was

taking care of everything.

DEREK

Derek paces the hospital hallway: He brought the kid here with a dislocated shoulder six months ago, and now a broken nose. The shoulder had been an accident: He'd jerked the boy up by one arm from the driveway into the car-seat. The hospital staff hadn't questioned him, just suggested he never try to lift a child by one arm again. There was a form to fill out, x-rays and a cast across the boy's chest, shoulder and down the arm.

This visit, however, required an hour-long interview with Social Services and a four page report that would remain on file at a child-welfare-office for the next ten years; not because of the cartilage damage so much as the bloody mouth. 23

DEREK AND FLORIDA

It was a shitty argument, Florida knew, but she couldn't stop herself. Derek's self-involvement had been hard to tolerate for the past two years, really. She had snuck up on her hatred of his cowardice and weak sex. Florida liked sneaky, though – it was her favorite way to handle any moron she came into contact with.

"You're a fucking waste of my time, you realize? I wish I'd never married you. I could have had my kids with anyone."

"The kids? Are you really that stupid? You think they would be these specific children without me? You really are an imbecile."

24 Florida just looked at him: He had no clue. Of course they would be the same kids.

DEREK

Pushing from behind and under the kid's butt up one of those wooden play-slide ladders, Derek feels a sudden rush of annoyance at the toddler-paced climb, and the smell of ripe diaper. He gives one hard shove, lifting the kid off the last rungs and up over the top. While his son slides face-first to the bottom, Derek stares at four tiny teeth embedded in the last wooden stair. 25

MARTIN

Martin watches the kid trying to maneuver a joystick around his new video-game. Martin has already beaten the game earlier in the week, but it's all this guy wants to do or talk about. Which kid is this? Martin can't quite remember. Their mothers are upstairs in the dining room reading tarot cards.

26   Oh, yes; *Kurt*, the kid's name is Kurt, and the mother is Laura Heavy; Mom's friend.

FLORIDA AND MARTIN

Laura is sure her husband is having an affair and has enlisted Florida's help in a quest for revenge. What Laura doesn't realize but Martin knows, is that Kurt's dad picks up his mom every Wednesday for an N.A. meeting that they never really go to. Martin knows because one Wednesday night he had been in the back seat of the neighbor's station wagon, driven home from a stage production of "*Oliver*" at the civic theater. He'd seen his mother and Kurt's dad kissing in a car at a stop light.

Florida is happy to lead Laura astray with tarot cards, astrological misinformation or palm readings.

FLORIDA

White heat presses the top of her head, black heat bubbles at her from the surface of tarmac. Florida feels a moment of small panic then steps off the corrugated stairway onto the landing strip. She continues cautiously, putting no weight onto her heels; the points would become stuck in melting tar as just before they would have been locked into metal holes in the stair steps.

It is Sunday and Florida has landed in Palm Springs for the funeral of her only remaining relative – Janine, a half-sister now dead of acute alcoholism. Seven years ago, when they had last spoken to one another at their grandmother's memorial service, Janine had drunkenly suggested that Florida not be overly sentimental: *When one has a heart of ice, one must remember to never allow melting, for then it is gone forever.*

Florida recalls laughing, knowing her heart as a far-removed ideomotor, nothing at all like ice.

JANINE

Hell was exactly where she lived; in the shadow her older half-sister left behind for her to wake toward.

When Florida had been home, Janine was perpetually stunned and lonely, but when Florida ran away, Janine became the focus of their mother's mania regarding angels and devils, souls squandered, beaten, eaten, sold and delivered to one fiery gate or another. In Janine's mind there was little to differentiate between good and evil activity.

When she turned eighteen, Janine made it a point to find her sister, who was now living in North Carolina, married and pregnant with the second boy.

At the time Janine felt no regrets for seducing Derek. He was so easy and obviously attracted to her. He told her she was better than her sister at everything.

DEREK

She'd planned the whole divorce: She would take the kids, she said. They'd argued and he'd threatened to have her arrested for kidnapping if she so much as packed one child-sized sock. She'd gotten a funny look on her face and then said, Yes, the boys should absolutely stay in their home.

She'd walked into their bedroom without another word and was gone in an hour. She had never left him before, and at first he imagined she would come back. After three months of no news, he started looking for her. She was nowhere.

Derek didn't go to the police because Florida had left with no intention of returning. Still, he thought she'd call to check on the boys. She had never called. Then her body was found a year ago.

FLORIDA

Florida was born with her eyes open. She projectile-vomited blood before her shoulders had been pushed out from between her mother's legs.

Linda, Florida's mother, killed herself when Florida was seventeen and pregnant.

Linda had been in therapy for several years and told Florida she planned suicide, that she'd explained in advance to her psychiatrist her reasons, including hatred for her daughter. Linda also told the doctor that Florida was Satan.

After her mother's funeral, Florida scheduled an abortion, then bought a plane ticket to Korea.

DEREK

He is supposed to be at his meeting, but is sitting at the Golden Editor drinking scotch; so much for the twelve little promises he'd committed to. Derek raises a private toast to his psychological counselor. He'd tried to tell the guy that this would never work: all of those words were not the way to end Derek's trouble.

Derek had been forced into a program after an incident at his job involving a senior executive at an awards luncheon. He had no memory of telling the guy to kiss his ass. He had been called to the Human Resource Department the next morning and informed of his requisite enrollment in a program to help him over-come addiction. He was made to understand that *"...continued employment at this company depended upon his successful completion of the program."*

Derek could say the words, do the dance, but it was all show and he knew it. There was an amusement factor in the idea that he had these people fooled, but it was wearing off. He was starting to be disgusted by the fact that folks were stupid enough to actually believe he was going to stop anything in order to keep a job.

He was just going to be more careful.

LINDA

Florida appeared at the top of the stairs dressed in a pretty yellow dress with a white daisy pattern around the hem. The child had first appeared in dirty short pants and a play shirt. She had stated that she was not coming to church today.

"Church is for cleanliness and presenting your best self to God. Get back upstairs and get ready."

These trials were daily battles between Linda and her daughter. Linda was beginning to wonder at God's wisdom in testing her so strenuously with this evil girl. She feared that someday soon the child would do something dreadful to her in her sleep.

Linda didn't like to think of it, but maybe this girl's soul was already consecrated to the devil instead of to God. If God was testing her with an impossible task, perhaps she was pre-destined to fail. She knew she did not love this child, but surely she could bring the girl to God's righteousness and make-up for her own lack.

FLORIDA

She furiously tugged her shirt off, yanked down her pants, ripped a dress off its hanger and pulled it on.

As she buckled the straps of the shiny black shoes she hated, she made a decision that changed her understanding of the world. She stood up, pulled off her under-pants and kicked them under the bed.

Maybe during Sunday School she'd pee on the rug where they sat while singing bible songs. 35

DEREK

It was a mistake to hit him with an open hand. The kid now had a red and blue handprint in the middle of his back.

Derek rubs his forehead with a closed fist; he can't miss work today – he has to take the kid to daycare. He knows they sometimes turn on a sprinkler and let the children run through the water to cool off on a hot afternoon.

"Do not take your shirt off today, understand?"

The boy just stares at him wetly with Florida's eyes.

MARTIN

The door opens – no, the window. It is David from the music store. Sometimes David has money to give Martin, sometimes David sucks him off for the dope. Martin doesn't really care either way.
Today is a blow, then Martin lights the pipe.

His mother comes from nowhere, literally; walks across the room and through the wall in the hallway. Martin gets up to follow her. He stops at the wall, puts his palms flat on the place where he watched her push through. He puts his forehead between his hands, tries to push himself into the wall to follow her. He hears her talking over there on the other side. He tries to hear what she says – he can't quite make out her instructions.

Martin begins to talk back to her. He has a list of questions.

DEREK

He's nervous pulling into the parking lot. What if those bitches noticed the kid's bruised back? And he's late again — they do not appreciate Derek's frequent tardiness in picking up the boy.

His son is asleep when he walks through the door. Derek picks him up to carry him to the car. Mrs. Ruiz gives him a look.

"Hola, Mr. Mom. He was tired today. Maybe he doesn't feel so good. No temperature, so we didn't call you to come take him home."

Derek assures her that he will tuck the kid in extra early tonight. He exits the building and pinches the boy's thigh as hard as he can. The kid just whimpers a little, doesn't wake up. Derek feels an overwhelming surge of annoyance at the lack of response.

FLORIDA

She knows it's too late not to have sex with him now. His tongue is in her mouth and tastes like smoked mozzarella, or maybe he puked a half hour ago. His knife blade is pressing hard on her collarbone.

She'd teased him and taken his extra cash for a week: he'd been in every night, obsessing over her, watching her. Florida knew the type and normally had them bounced after a couple of times, but she'd decided to take this one riding a few extra rounds. He was contributing nicely to her ticket-home collection plate.

He'd caught up to her right as she was putting her key into the locked doorknob of her apartment door. His knife was out in one hand, his other hand covered her mouth and nose.

"Go on – open up."

DEREK

The kids were both long asleep. Derek dialed the number on the unfolded paper he'd planned to get rid of the last time he used it. He stayed five hours the first time he bought in – just enough to forget her, he thought. He knew he would stay longer tonight; he'd have to. The last time had taught him that he'd have to hit a lot harder if he really meant to murder all thoughts of her forever.

40   He'd be home again before the boys were up for cereal.

MARTIN

Martin watches for any sign of change. He believes his mother has evaporated from her body to enter the sky, through which she will send messages in the form of weather patterns.

Martin knows the weather is a source of change, and that clouds bear witness to these changes. He thinks his dead mother may be indicating her displeasure or approval through various shifts in cloud structure.

Today he sees a plane sew silently in and out of a white mountain; a needle sparkling minutely, far gone into its own disappearance.

SONANT

o o o

Last night a falsely curbed
horizon slipped the sun
into black-silt water.
Noon today, a boy asks his father

Is godzilla bigger than heaven?
"Sometimes," swallows another
mouthful of young walking in
man toward tomorrow faces.

Monster stars under all the darkness, bites the sky out
in blind doses, its shadow on
the ground – a flat universe;

characters in a very low living,
living where there is no day.

45

o o o

Day looks in the tower
where time won't stay.
"Time is nutser than a dingo,"
noon today.

The boy won't participate.
The earth won't open.
He'll watch in slow motion.
The earth won't open

his dreaming: Watch the shadow
meet a body and crawl
into the space of heaven
under the heavy belly

of itself. Some things get
lost in their finding.

o o o

Finding twelve, he understands
words he heard Dad tell someone:
"The mocking birds are shitting blood from all the nests

in the mulberry." Noon today,
boy walks to a pond. He's watched
a dead crow bloat for weeks.
He wants it to burst — see what flew

under the feathers when he stabs...
The carcass moves away pushing
a path through stagnant water.
He hopes it will break

before winter — before the ice
air slows its swelling

o o o

Bulbs full of light and insects on
a screen slaps. Mother buries
flowers by the front porch
again today noon closes one eye

a boy lights her head in flash white
he practices his shooting
lifts his arm into a swarm of small flies. He is shooting her

the old-lady way. He is
in and out of the woods here
she disappears into what
he has already made dead.

She is just moving tissue.
She never knows his true response.

o o o

She wipes his lip with the back of her wrist; his blood again –
her pale skin, blue veins. Another scarlet horizon hangs
   in all her windows.

She believes he is
a most human extremity
at the top of mortality –
a lesion through clouds.

Noon today she lifts him
by his throat to the door he is
locked out until she remembers to watch a long dream of him

crying so she hates the sound.
He hasn't cried in three years

49

○ ○ ○

Anger rains off the dark leaves;
Cherry the last tree holding.
51 minutes to Dayton, noon today,
air mobbed with flying.

The boy combs his head for static.
At the funeral a crowd of words:
Love ye one another. Dead looks
alive stuffed into dumb magic;

bones are tight pushing skin
like fat hands push black umbrellas
in and out along the headstones,
the boy feels his past

prayers move under the dark bandage over a sore opening at last

○ ○ ○

In the boy's heart a knife holds still;
it is his mother who
won't allow him to move without
pain – today he's killed

in his head loving her,
he breathes in the shallows trying not to survive under the river –
    oxygen is a waiting room:

Air means less to the corpse
than a sharp silver flash
moves like fish to eat
anything dead in the water flesh

breaking apart feels all over
open to the pressure of quiet.

o o o

Father hung a dead carp curled on a glue seal, while alive
    pulled a long line with his dark mouth. The pond laps toward
miracle, stirs the moon

a scrap of evidence in decoration.
If he tries a boy will know patterns hidden on the water surface are
    predictable, targets for him to use

in the pond. Steps fall away from
their footprints, the surface leaves mirror deeper dancing and
drowning remains reckless in the deep.

His heart lives in water – drops
like a bullet … he will close one eye.

o o o

High on the house with an umbrella
a boy steps on air
confident in the large
nature of a twisted storm

noon today his fall
will matter to trusted legs,
perfect bone.
The storm plays with sticks.

He wakes to pink bleeding on green
grass. The rain makes mud
sick sounds, nothing scares him
more than this waking –

the idea he is not dead. Inside
the house, walls hold together.

53

Thanks to Lord Dermond,
Chip Bunker, Amy Mayhem,
boni & tobi joi, OTPP, John Yau,
John R. and Elizabeth, Dr. Peddu,
and to inspirational artists:
William Faulkner, Baudelaire,
David Foster Wallace,
JT LeRoy and many others...

Ronna Lebo is a poet, painter, and musician living in Brooklyn, New York. She received her MFA from Mason Gross School of the Arts, and teaches in fine arts at Kean University, New Jersey. She is the co-author of four music CDs, two poetry anthologies, and one poetical memoir. She founded Ocular Press – an imprint featuring hand-made books of poetry. She also co-founded and edits titles for Off The Park Press, a non-profit publisher of poetry. She has performed as Alice B. Talkless in the greater New York area.

Prolapse is composed in Interstate, a typeface designed by Tobias Frere-Jones. Topaz is used for the titling, and was created by Jonathan Hoefler. Thomson-Shore printed and bound the edition in Dexter, Michigan.